what a wonderful world it would be if only we'd give it a chance. Love baby, love. That's the secret." The message through the words can be interpreted in many ways. But the message through the emotions, the concern, the pain and the hurt in his voice from everything that was going on wrong in the society, that message is still echoing in the atmosphere. If only people would have the heart and the ear to listen to it.

Then there is this, one of the greatest singers from India, a living legend MADHURANIJI, who is a one of her kind classical GHAZAL singer. Her rendition of one of her melodious songs "YEH DAAG-DAAG UJAALA, YEH SHAB GHAZEEDA SEHAR". It was written by a great and renowned Indian poet ALAMA IQBAL. To describe the poem in a few words would be something like this. It's about a country (the land) speaking to its people about the condition they have brought upon it even after the war against the oppressors is over and the country is independent finally. A country that has just won its freedom at the cost of seeing the corpses of millions of humans and animals, children, young, and old, men and women, civilians and soldiers. These corpses are a result of civil unrest and war between the people of the same country in the name of discriminations of color, caste, religion and culture. "This unclear brightness with uncanny, scary patches of darkness within it. This condition of the morning after the war for freedom, the smoky, foggy, painfully hurting morning, is not the state which I had desired for as the reward for the sacrifices of millions of young brave hearts who could've otherwise, just like many others out there, enjoyed the joys and the pleasures of youthfulness. People are cutting the throats of other people to prove their supremacy over others. The greed and selfishness of some merciless tyrant people with no remorse has given these stains to our mornings and our evenings. This is not the result for which I dreamt about freedom." The pain and the hope of seeing things change around us, that her voice expresses is exactly like what she says, "why is it so difficult for us all to co-exist with all our individual qualities and natures of diversities and inhibitions. The world is big enough to accommodate all of us. So what exactly are we human beings fighting for?"

We may have come to believe that the days of KINGS and LORDS have long passed and are over. We may also love to believe that the world is free from TYRANT DICTATORS and RULERS. But the truth is, neither have they gone anywhere, nor we are free. Yes the titles, faces and presentation forms have definitely changed. The level of success with their tyrant ways has dropped a lot in comparison to what it used to be. But if only you could notice the sufferings from today's prevailing systematically orchestrated tyranny in disguise of racism, and other discriminations, and if only you could hear the silent cries of the indirectly and covertly oppressed people in our society even today! Dictators, cruel and brutal tyrants of yesterday and of today are not known to have remorse or regrets about your agony and pain that humans have suffered physically and emotionally from their acts.   We do know about some of the very famous tyrant people who walked this earth, but there are many more and they have continued to come from time to time and have left their marks and scars on the face of our society. Remember Caligula? The Roman Emperor who lived from 37AD till 41AD, better referred to as THE PERVERT CEASAR. He did not care if his subjects or people specially women hated him for being as pathetically cruel, dominant and brutal as he was. All he cared about was that he was able to establish fear in everybody's hearts. His motto "Let them hate, so long as they fear". He was so notorious for his sexual Bacchanalias and insatiable lust that he did not ever hesitate to take the women that he wanted even if it meant to take them away from their husbands. Caligula declared himself a living god. History is witness that tyrants' lives have been very short lived. Caligula ended by way of assassination.

How about the legendary tyrant Mongolian emperor known as the supreme warrior known as GENGIS KHAN. He was the founder and the ruler of the Mongol Empire from 1206 till 1227. Although he was not directly subjecting tyranny over the general public his policies followed by his men made day to day humans suffers to extremity in many countries like China, Central Asia and across Eastern Europe, and for a very short period even India with little success and influence.

There were many other evil tyrants who have left their impact in the lives of humans in many different regions of the earth. However the most widely spread conquerors and rulers in the modern times were the BRITISH. Nobody has had the kind of influence, and impact on human minds and lives as the British. Their ways were completely different and very systematically they would divide societies and communities to establish their rules. Today also most political parties in almost every country use the DIVIDE AND RULE policy that was laid originally by the British. The impact and the scars in the form of aftermath of their cruelty and brutality and the influences from divisions of humans that they created are still alive all over the world. The wounds from the wrath of DISCRIMINATION that the world is suffering from are still fresh and have yet not been healed. In fact today's politicians secretly continue to use them in disguise even today as strategies and weapons to govern and rule people in many countries.

Over the period of billions of years, several super continents have formed and broken up, as a result of churning and circulation in the Earth's mantle. This is how the seven continents of the earth came to be. After the breaking up of the Pangea, the process of shifting of plate tectonics has not yet stopped. The shapes of continents and relatively the shape of countries, in fact even some states within some countries have undergone changes as a result of plate tectonics. This has also resulted in migration of humans, animals, birds and even plants and insects from one region to another. New climatic cycles and conditions for survival went on to change the biology and psychology of many species.

Many life forms, including many human like species also, were forced to go extinct after migration due the unsuitable new climatic and environmental conditions. While many new life forms evolved also. This is why some animals are found everywhere, while some may only be in the Southern Hemisphere, and others only in the Western Hemisphere, etc. For migration even though humans had their two feet, they forced to get innovative and one of the earliest inventions was to help humans to travel across water, Boats. One the humans settled down in their new regions, the biological differences began to evolve and the relative changes became too obvious on their appearances like their skin tones, shapes and sizes of their facial features, their height etc. Different humans experienced different types of changes different climates. The interbreeding among groups of people of the same region, generation after generation went on to establish a unique human race. Racial differences bear more complex than just differences in skin color and hair texture.

While modern science claims that the difference between human DNA and Chimpanzees is a little over one percent, I disagree with their theory. There certainly are similarities but the percentage and ratios and the proportions of the elements that comprise the genetic formation and the DNA of humans is far too different than the chimpanzees. There are many elements missing in the DNAs of the chimpanzees. If we had evolved from the chimpanzees or any other human like animal then when and why would the process of evolution stop? The process of evolution is an ongoing and a never ending process. All life form continues to evolve in some way. Firstly the notion that all humans came out of Africa itself is wrong. The color of the skin of humans is created by special cells called melanocytes. In the areas of the earth which is dominated mostly by dry climate and scarcity of water, hence less greenery the skin works harder to protect an individual from the harmful effects of the UV rays and other attacks from the open natural space. It works completely in a more moist and cooler climatic region. Look at it this way when its sunny and bright the glare from the light hurts your eyes, but then as you wear sunglasses that effect is gone. The skin cells in a living species are naturally programmed via the brain to act in a way according to the needs of the climatic conditions in a region. Over the period the out energies and other elements which the skin accepts and adds it into as one of our inseparable natural genetic components, it becomes the unique identifier of that individual.

The beginning of the historical era witnessed territories and countries formed and designated and then legislations and constituencies were formed. This was done to ensure the wellbeing of mankind in a particular region based upon the social and the cultural natural of the habitants of the region. But the most important consideration was the humans right of equality. In a country nobody would be considered superior to anybody. Yes there maybe superiority in the social status resulting from one's success from their personal merits and earnings. But in the eyes of the country, in the name of God all humans will be considered equal regardless of their social status, race, ethnicity, color, language, culture or religion.

However soon the constitutionally and the legislatively established morals in the society began being challenged by the personal objectives, ideologies and practices of a few communities within the society. This has not stop until this day even though the country is divided in to small and large fragments of territories with different societies and communities who are each individually trying to prove the superiority, excellence and worthiness to be higher than the others. This is what brought about and has maintained discriminations of various kinds in the human society. But the discriminatory issues got highlighted and gained prominence more and more with the rising of the race for technological excellence and advancements between different communities and regions and countries.

The basic human nature is progressive which is lead by thirst and greed to excel. This is what gave birth to and rise to the race to procure mass amounts of gold which would allow them to hold as much power over the emerging human population as possible. We are definitely aware that gold has been the most significant source and is to this day the central and the most essential requirement which determines a country's advancement of human population in a region. However in current times the constantly emerging and developing technology has captured the market and has become the deciding factor of the percentage and the nature of economic growth of a country, Gold may not exactly have the same significance as it did in the past and it may not be the only source of advancement of a country.

Today technology has become a vital need for the modern era. We cannot even envisage a world without technology. But talk to the grand parents and their parents and they will tell you to remember that there was a time where people used to live without today's technology and if you may compare with the quality of life, even though today's generation may find it highly objectionable and questionable and may even say it's all about your perspective, the elders will tell you that their childhood was much closely linked and related with their families, friends and   NATURE and purity than today's generation's childhood. It's not that then there was absolutely no technology. It is the thirst or the greed to excel using advancement and development to get empowered by leaving behind the others who may still be struggling to survive and easily put down by the more advanced and better developed people. This race of advancement has created division in the human societies and has given birth to many discriminations.

Technological advancements and developments were in view of promoting a new movement of growth with an intention of social and humanitarian reforms. Neither technology nor development is bad. It's the use of these which is either good or bad. Technology does improve the economic conditions of a country. It also empowers a country and makes others to look up to them as leaders. Development boosts the ego of a country. Take for instance the war machinery. Different types of advanced automated guns, fighter planes, ships, etc. But to use these you need to have enemies also. So you use it to impress others so that they may buy from you and boost the growth of your economy. This is the simplest way to explain the use of power to manipulate the world around you. But the enmity creates hostility and hatred towards one another not only between countries but also among people in a mixed society where people from different cultural backgrounds and values live together.

We all know it too well that we have severe social issues in our society. These issues have existed for too long for us to not realize the need to resolve it. But what is it that continues to keep these issues alive??? Even though as citizens of the same country, the fact is that the country is formed by the union of people from different cultural and social nature. We live in a MIXED SOCIETY with people who hail from different societies, communities, religious beliefs, different cultural backgrounds etc from around the world. We cannot remain ignorant of the fact that we humans are TERRITORIAL. It's not just the dogs and cats and other animals that are territorial. But we have the intelligence which the other species do not have. We realized the need for becoming cultured and civilized while the other animals cannot do that. This among many other aspects makes us superior to the other species.

The social issues which generally crop up from the threat from violent trendies which are portrayed by people with their challenging attitude and unreasonable behavior. People often ignore the need to approach an ongoing issue in a positive way to find a solution to resolve the issue. But people either find it easy to blame the offender, or their intelligence is just too blocked in anger so they continue with their ways and the problem continues to exist in our society. We are responsible for keeping the flames of these issues burning. But enough is enough. This flame is spreading and engulfing the human race and dividing us even more than ever before. The most prominent of all other social issues is DISCRIMINATION. The beauty of diversity is being abused and challenged and the colors of the rainbow are being destroyed and shattered. It's time now to stand up step forward and heal the WOUNDS OF COLOR.

The moment the word discrimination is mentioned immediately the western society or the white people pop up in people's minds in general. But that's not fair and its definitely not justified to put the entire blame upon any one race of humans. Discrimination and prejudice exist all over the world. Look at India and China. In India, there are still many communities that are known as UNTOUBALES. What about the FEMALE FETUS being killed in the womb even before they are developed for WANT of a MALE baby? There are so many castes, religious diversities and class differences based on the social status. In fact they have used mythology and involved GOD to endorse the discriminations which they practice.

Now let us look at China. Even though the constitution of the People's Republic of China clearly states that all citizens are equal and that ethnic minorities, people with religious beliefs, and women should not be discriminated against in any aspect of civil life, including employment. There's nothing new about the fact that WOMEN in China are the most discriminated people. If a woman and a man apply for the same job at the same time, the man is given preference over men. This is applicable in fields of SCIENCE & TECHNOLOGY, ENGINEERING, MEDICAL, TEACHING, POLICE, MILITARY you name it. Women are forced to face rejection, denial and prejudice.

The foremost truth and the important point to note about DISCRIMINATION and INTOLERANCE wherever it is practiced is that it is the most prominent and obvious form of human rights violations and abuse. It is a rejection of people whom we perceive as different. A denial for the rights of others to have respect for their cultural practices and beliefs based upon one's consideration of one's own beliefs, practices to be the only rightful one.

While people travel from their country of birth to other countries to shape or to re-shape their fate and to improve their life conditions. They face the least expected, Discrimination problems. People are discriminated on various grounds like; because of their age, due to disability, their ethnicity, their origin, their political belief, their skin color, religion, sex or gender, sexual orientation, language, culture and on many other grounds. All this when we all continue to do our best to survive and to evolve and be able to contribute our part to our human society.

It is however obvious that wherever there will come together humans from different backgrounds, and interact with each other there's bound to be clash of ideology, understanding, disagreements etc. There will also be competition between people and between groups of people on many different issues. It's very much like in a school, children do have differences among each other and eventually the teacher or the principal intervenes to sort out the issues. But imagine if the PRINCIPAL is involved in treating one of the students on the basis of the student's race, or ethnicity, or gender or skin color, then what would be the first reaction of the student? HELPLESSNESS. This is how the victims of RACISM feel. The discrimination does not always have words or a voice. But actions and sometimes even gestures are louder than words and voice.

DISCRIMINATION with intent to harm has been practiced for too long for us humans to not realize the impact and the nature of harm on the victims' psychology. Its a curse for humans and for humanity and we know it and yet we have willingly allowed it to exist in our society to this day. Only the victims can know how it feels to be discriminated against and how much it hurts. But what's even more hurtful is to know that there are such humans who have no remorse or regrets about the torturous acts they perform on their fellow humans. By committing brutal and atrocious crimes against another one of their own kind, only because they are different in appearance or because they are less fortunate than you and therefore you enjoy a better social status than them, is barbaric no matter how civilized you may claim to be.

Human race has come a long way. The changes in human appearances are a result of systematic step by step but with gradual pace of time, process, which took effect based upon the ever changing life conditions via nature. In the ancient world there were many other creatures that were human like. Neanderthals bore the closest physical resemblances and other patterns and features to humans. Of course the cross breeding of the similar human like species between them and with humans resulted in more different types of human races. Many of the ancient human races that were the products of cross breeding went extinct with time. Mostly due to improper and unbalanced biological and chemical formation. But the races of humans that did survive and evolved from then to future times established themselves into different societies and communities in different parts of the world. Then of course the climatic variations in different regions of the earth further designed and formed the physical appearance of humans. However the social nature, behavioral nature and the nature of instincts were established in humans based on the availability of resources needed for survival.

Discriminations exist in all communities of TERRITORIAL animals or creatures, including humans. But it is practiced by some humans to extremity to give extremely horrendous results and consequences. The diversities which make our existence so beautiful and was given to all animals by the creator like COLOR, VARIATION IN OUR UNDERSTANDING, AND OUR INTELLIGENCE, THE POWER TO COMMUNICATE (LANGUAGE), ETHNICITY(TERRITORY), PHYSICAL APPEARANCE, CULTURE etc, but sadly these diversities some humans converted into tools and reasons to divide, discriminate and create feud. Forget about religion, our human intelligence and our realization should be sufficient to help us know that while our social nature, dressing, appearance, language, color are different, we are still the same SPECIES, all of us are HUMAN BEINGS. Beneath the skin, our formation is exactly the same. It's not like some humans have two hearts while some have only one. Or some humans have two brains while some have only one. Why are the biological variations made into tools to divide us and oppress and suppress some humans by some humans? Let us explore and try to understand what are the factors and elements that continue to sustain these differences and convert them into dangerous tools and weapons of destruction of peace and harmony in our society.

The term YOU ARE WHAT YOU EAT or ONE MAN'S FOOD IS ANOTHER MAN'S POISON are not new to us. The reason behind such phrases is that the FOOD that we consume apparently does have a very big impact and effect on the biology and on psychology of every individual. It's a different thing that we never seem to realize so we don't come to know or even doubt of the effects from eating what we do. This is clearly proved by some people being ALLERGIC to some TYPES OF FOOD ITEMS. Or some people falling ill by eating some types of food. Fruits, Seeds/grains, leafy and other types of Vegetables, sea products, meat etc provide essential nutrients and minerals that we need to survive. But these products continuously keep resulting in changes to the different types of cells in our body. These constant changes continue to give various results to our entire existence like our psychology, nature, feelings, tastes, likes, dislikes, temperaments, and OUR SKIN. Emotions that are a result of BIOLOGICAL and CELLULAR formation are the ones that are responsible for the formation of the nature of psychology in a person. The energies that we take from nature are not out of choice or option. They are deposited into our system by nature based on what type of energies our thoughts and feelings invoke or attract.

We know that the Bees and the Butterfly go from plant to plant to perform the pollination process. They collect pollen from one plant and fly to another which they get attracted to and deposit it, then pick pollen from there and fly to yet another plant. This process continues on for ever. Similarly are humans who migrate from their birth country to other countries carrying their cultural heritage, traditions and customs etc. As they colonize and settle down in the new country they deposit their traditions, culture, language, religious beliefs etc in the new country. But what humans ignore is the question of how welcomed or unwelcomed are their deposits in the new country. This is because when you make a home you feel comfortable to live as you will. You take your freedom for granted to continue to live just the way you did in your own country. Now if the migration is done to a land of the free, then the question of being welcomed or unwelcomed does not arise at all. It's just that you will have to share the land with those who made this land their home before you. However because we humans also like the cats and dogs are territorial many a times acceptance of anything new is not easily possible.

America in particular is a country of immigrants. Everyone living here today has hailed from some other country at some point in time. Some came before the others and some came after the others. The beauty of this country is its diversity. Diversity brings together different types of intelligence and evolves better life conditions and creates a much developed society. These societies offer better system and a multicultural environment for better life conditions. With combined intelligence, new and robust opportunities are created for everyone. Everybody came to America to live that dream which was probably next to impossible in their own under developed and not so systematic, poverty stricken country. But even if they have come out of their country, they have not completely alienated the community where they were born. They remain attached to their cultural heritage and continue to maintain the love for the practices of their customs and rituals. This is why people from similar cultural background mostly choose to live where their own kinds are in majority. There's nothing wrong with it.

But what's wrong is that when somebody from another culture enters your area he/she is treated with disrespect and is subjected to racial slurs, comments and discriminative treatment. Why? That person is as human as anybody else. So why must he/she suffer prejudice?

Every country's constitution is designed with all legislative provisions and enriched with respectful core values for human lives and care, compassion and consideration, fairness and justice to all humanity. These points have been well studied and well calculated and with careful consideration have been respectfully recorded as amendments in our constitutional transcripts. So why are we witnessing and reading news flashes and seeing on television the latest uproar against racial discrimination? Its not about black or white, it is about black and white and Asians, Hispanics etc. Like as if the religious discrimination was not enough already. We have been suffering the brunt of religious discrimination in the form of TERROR ATTACKS and MASS KILLINGS by radical extremists. We are not able to handle the consequences of ONE DISCRIMINATION but due to our carelessness we continue to create more and more?

   Racism in different parts of the world is of different style and nature. Racism exists in almost every country in the world. The reasons may be whatever, but the BOTTOM LINE TRUTH is that humans hate humans. When Indians migrate to other countries, they don't just drain out their understandings and notions. There are differences and discriminatory realizations that are deeply entrenched in their psychological system like caste system, stereotypes and prejudices and xenophobia and are rampant in India. In fact why only caste system? There are other issues like sub-castes too (gotras), then there are Dalits, the Harijans, Brahmins, Baniyas etc. What about the dining taboos that are based on caste? people from one community cannot sit parralel to people of another community. They cannot eat with the people of other caste and cannot marry with people from other caste. These closed communities are naturally full of prejudices towards *the other*, the outsider. Every state considers itself superior. This phenomenon is global, like Polish, Italian jokes in America. Or English, Irish, Welsh, Scottish jokes in the UK. Or Indian jokes about South Indians and Sardars, etc. We humorously but mercilessly categorise and divide each other.

  Yes the RACISM in India is different from the western concept, but racism is racism. However, even so they conveniently ignore all that they practice in their country of birth or origin, and and stand up to complain, object and protest against similar discrimination when they are subjected to and are targeted by people from other countries outside India.

  As recently as on May 27th, Masonda Ketanda Olivier, an African settled in India, was beaten to death by some Indians over hiring of an AUTORIKSHAW. He was a Congolese national waiting for an autorikshaw where others were waiting for it too. He was confronted by a mob of men late at night last Friday in New Delhi. They made racial slurs and passed racial remarks which lead to a fight and they killed him. Of course the Police investigated and found out that the incident was due to a dispute over the hiring of an autorickshaw. But Olivier's friend, an Ivorian national said that it was a clear case of hate crime, with racial epithets repeatedly invoked. Olivier was about 24 years of age and taught French in a local School in India.

What about the ongoing problems in Japan about racism? The country's society and government are permeated by a narrative that says people must "look Japanese" before they can expect equal treatment in society. In Japan, the nature of racism is slightly different, but then again racism is racism. They base their treatment and behavior towards others based on the some very obvious facts like skin color, whether one speaks Japanese or not, whether or not one knows and respects the Japanese culture. They have many other insidious varieties of racism that are sprouted from hate.

While the case of racial profiling with white Americans, Europeans or British is relatively benign in Japan, the other ethnic groups suffer a lot more. People who are from African descend (or anybody who is dark skinned), other Asians (in particular SE Asians and Asians from former Japanese colonies), or minorities within Japan such as the Ainu of Hokkaido, the Ryukyu of Okinawa, ethnic Koreans and the Burakumin betray far more negative stereotypes.

Japan doesn't have civil rights legislation which would penalizes racial discrimination by citizens or businesses. In some cases, businesses openly discriminate. For example, apartment ads may say "Japanese only". Racism is not considered a crime in Japan so the government does not keep any track of racial incidents. Its because of this that Japanese nationals are subjected to racial problems outside of Japan specially in other Asian countries.

How about Chinese, who are extremely proud of their culture and consider themselves to be of a superior race compared to any other human race. Every Chinese believes he can out-think his foreign colleagues due to his unmatched level of intelligence. A little darkness is ok but in China, the general theory is if you are dark skin toned then you are to be afraid of. Specially looking at African people they immediately remember of crimes, violence, rape, etc.

The major reason which constitutes to racism against Africans who may be living in any part of the world is from the general understanding and belief by the white people around the world and this long and ugly tradition of treating Africans as savage animals and the African continent to be the dirtiest, diseased place to be feared of. This understanding prevails only because most of Africa is poor and poverty struck so it's thought to be as a dirty and diseased place. This needs to be changed. The humans from the rest of the world must step forward and compassionately be generous to help uplift the lives of the poor living in unfavorable life conditions in every country. So that their souls are not made to suffer the agony of being considered unworthy of existing on this planet. All humans of every race are human beings. Judging people based on how people in their country live in wrong. First of all people who are targets of your racial slurs are no longer living amidst the people of their country in that condition. Secondly because they did not want to continue to deal with and suffer those conditions so they chose to migrate to other parts of the earth. But they did not do so to become subjects and targets of harsh and hurtful discriminations. Thirdly every human tries to with all available resources to make their environment and life conditions better. Just because the environmental and climatic conditions in your region are better than other regions it does not make you a superior race.

Even though Australia has a culture of denial when it comes to racism, in work places racism has been in practice beyond any measure. But the seed of racism is sowed in the little minds when they are introduced to racism in schools. Even today in Australia, one in every five schools, students experience racism. Be it the field of sports or other academic programs. Right from the teachers to the local students, throw racial slurs at people and put down people based on their country of origin and based on their color, ethnicity, language and religion. Its not always only physical acts of discrimination. There are also verbal racial abuse where the victim is tortured with words. The effects of racism and discrimination can only be negative. The white supremacists are so prominently powerful that in a society like Australia's, one cannot get much support standing up and voicing against racism.

Australia is not alone in being so prominent with its open practices of racial discrimination. We may often hear about Arabs or People from Islamic countries being harassed and targeted with religious discrimination in countries around the world specially these sic major European countries like Slovenia, Romania, Slovakia, Austria, Hungary and the Czech Republic. But what is generally overlooked is the discrimination practices in the Arab countries against the non-Muslims. The people with white skin may still not be victimized with racism. But if you are not a white skin, then God help you. Specially if you are a non-Muslim from Either, India, China, Nepal, Bangladesh or Sri Lanka. These people are treated as if they are unworthy of even being alive.

The countries that are so deeply into hovering racism often forget that those who are victimized are often treated as fuel to be burned in the front line in times of problems and major social issues. The truth that they also make a vital contribution, through their research, to solving many of society's most pressing issues are conveniently ignored and forgotten.

Its a tragedy that today inequality is not considered worth being concerned about by many people who rush to fast paced economically growing countries. In the powerful countries, the main focus is on either the race of MILITARY ADVANCEMENTS or ECONOMIC DEVELOPMENT, so many of the social issues remain active until they blow up out of proportion on the face of the governments. We the people in the developed

countries are truly blessed and must be thankful to have all the advanced and greatly developed technologies in different fields like medical field,
engineering field, and software development field etc. Many of our basic needs are better fulfilled today than what they were in the times of our parents' childhood. But the problems that were major in the childhood days of our parents are even bigger issues today and we are not able to stop the growth of these problems.

Some of the reason why racism and other discriminatory problems in our society are growing more and more are that, to advance in life and to take advantage of the opportunities in today's ever advancing and technologically boosting world, people accept
to compromise with their self respect and honor and in want of better and comfortable financial status in their lives, they have developed an attitude of "we don't mind facing with these problems". They leave their home countries and travel to other countries knowing that they will have to face and bear with discriminations. They leave their countrymen

and women to suffer because their country is unable to offer them the life that they can enjoy in other developed and wealthy countries. Did you know that there are over 500,000 women and girls who die due to complications related to pregnancy and childbirth every year out of which over 99 percent of those deaths occur in developing countries such as Indonesia, Philippines, Bangladesh, Pakistan, Kenya, Tanzania and other African countries and in rural India. From among those that are born, many a times they are born with physical disabilities or deficiency. This is because of lack of proper medical faculties and because very few medical practitioners who are thoroughly knowledgeable and well experienced, agree to remain behind to serve their own people. Most of the knowledgeable professionals choose to migrate to other countries even if they are made to feel that they are not welcome there. They choose to become targets of racial slurs and victims of inequality. This is the responsibility of the governments of those countries which have to provision for immigrants to start afresh in their country, to secure and protect their rights, self respect, dignity and honor.

The silence of some people who continue to bear with the torture from racism and treatments of inequality only encourages the oppressors to victimize more and more people.

Frustration from realizing the incompetence in oneself which is the cause of failure and discontentment often hurts a person's ego deep within even if the person may not realize it. But its not always inferiority complex which invokes racism. It is also superiority complex which makes people behave inappropriately. One gets filled inside with anger, jealousy, vengeance, against those who have better life conditions. Based upon their personal evaluation about a community or a society of people, people suffering from superiority complex based on their understanding create an image of others to be less than in comparison to what they believe about themselves to be. Many a times such understandings lead some people to believe about others to be unworthy of the comforts, position and powers that others enjoy. People practicing racism refuse to or hesitate to give to others the credit of their efforts, hard work, dedication and determination with which they achieved what they did. This is because of the belief in many people that they are of a superior race. They just believe that they have more rights on everything in life including success, comfort, position and power. They are not able to make themselves to respect the fact that other races are also capable of achieving that which these people have been believing to be solely and rightfully theirs and only theirs. A great example to explain these facts better is the life of our very own President Barak Obama.

It's an undeniable truth that racism did not spare even the president of the greatest country on earth, USA, President Barak Obama. The initial days of his term as a president faced many odds and challenges posed by the congress. Presidency in USA has always been dominated by the white people. Even though the founding fathers of America clearly stipulated the rights of equality in our constitution, and even though USA proudly proclaims and glorifies it's strength to be the rights of equality, and its diversity, it is a well known fact that the white supremacy made sure for 100s of years that nobody else, other than a WHITE MAN, ever becomes the president of USA. During the tenure as the president, Obama created history after history. Not just the fact that an African American became the president of UNITED STATES OF AMERICA, but also with his intelligence and his considerate, unbiased patriotic policies, his understanding, patience and tolerance he reinstated the honor and respect of America and Americans in the eyes of the people around the world who had almost broken off their ties with USA considering Americans to be the most arrogant and uncaring bullies of the world. He created history by changing many hearts around the world including in USA of even some of the strongest white racist Americans who initially were absolutely against an African American or anybody else becoming the president of USA. The congress which is lead by majority of white people posed obstacles and hurdles to make him unpopular among people and to ensure his failure. But he remained firm on his path. Today people from every race, people from all walks of life and people from every country around the world respect and honor this great man with the highest regards.

However the truth is that if the president of United States of America, the most powerful person in the world, is also not spared from racism then how can a regular human being be spared? The question is not about the act itself. The question is about who houses and preserves HATE FOR HUMAN BEINGS because others do not look like them in color, language, social mannerisms, customs or culture? The question is also about what is every individual doing about this issue. It's a problem and everyone knows that. The problem is psychological and it cannot be solved or changed overnight. We need to trace our steps as far back as possible and reach to the root cause of this problem. But of course with the intention of resolving it.

The class system and slavery that was created by the English people traveled with them to all lands all over the earth that was conquered by the English people. They deposited their beliefs, systems, mannerisms, and laws wherever they went and left it there as their signature when they left that land. The forward generations continue to the practice of beliefs and customs and rituals that were established by the previous generations. Even many of those who later on in their life became great leaders, in their childhood have witnessed slaves and maid services being abusively employed. They witnessed discriminations of different types that were in practice in America from the time when America was still being formed. With time their intelligence and the nature of reasoning found a way to justify and establish those beliefs and practices, which included color and class discriminations, as a part of life. In fact their belief became so confirmed that they began to believe that opposing them was unfair and wrong, because they believed that those who suppressed were meant to be. It's because of this that they behaved with slaves, maids and poor with disrespect, inconsiderable and careless attitude. There have been discriminations of many kinds that have existed in the human society from the beginning of history. However COLOR discrimination is definitely one of the oldest one practiced by the western society. Recorded historic facts provide enough evidence of the oppression and tyranny that humans have been subjected to in the name of color. while there have been many protests and riots which have resulted into mass killings and social problems etc, the oppressors and the tyrant kinds have managed to maintain their reign and supremacy and have managed to keep the discrimination alive to this day and time. But it astonishing that even though there are more supporters of people who are discriminated against than the number of people who discriminate yet this nature in some humans of abusing humanity remains as one of the largest problems in our society even today. So who is responsible for storing this problem and from time to time bringing it out in the open to create social unrest?

Such discriminations were used as tools and weapons majorly by politicians who covertly orchestrated, guided and controlled the nature of incidents and of course the results. However at least in the past the law enforcement department was always there to put things back in order. But in recent times the discrimination problem has spread and engulfed the minds, hearts and psychology of even the police! This is really tragic, worrisome and very concerning. ARMY, POLICE, MEDICAL PROFESSIONALS, JUDICIAL AUTHORITIES etc are where helpless humans store their HOPE. Hope for PROTECTION, SAFETY, MEDICAL HELP and JUSTICE etc. These authorities are considered the most powerful bodies and only below GOD. Where should people go if they are denied help and failed by their protectors and are subjected to prejudice by these authorities?

When one speaks about RACIAL DISCRIMINATION one immediately pictures an AFRICAN AMERICAN or SOMEONE WHO IS NOT WHITE. To many this may come as a surprise, but the truth is that racism is not only practiced by WHITES. At least not in America. In USA its also practiced against WHITES. Take this case of Texas university for instance. This discrimination centered around a white, female student who was denied admission to the University of Texas. The student, Abigail Fisher, said she was unfairly discriminated against because she was white. Even though the U.S. law prohibits racial discrimination in general, and the State government is required to safeguards the rights of the general public and ensure the practice rights of equality to maintain the integrity of democracy, University of Texas in today's time and era has a policy that uses race as a factor for admissions! Then there's this case of a white police officers who was denied the job because of African-American majority and was told on his face that he should not even bother applying because the chief was trying to get a color officer down to the department. Some days later for real an African-American women was appointed at the job. So the point is that today DISCRIMINATION has become a weapon or a tool to get even by taking revenge. Here's yet another case of racial prejudice, This incident occurred in the Alabama suburb, where a 57years old grandfather who had come to USA to visit his children and grand children and was taking an evening walk in his neighborhood. CCTV footage showed he was confronted by two police officers who nabbed him and threw him to the ground. The reason for suspecting him to be dangerous was his Indian attire. That incident has left him paralyzed ever since. There are many cases that continue to occur in different states of USA even today. For example there was this case, a complaint that was filed by the EEOC against a Texas-based oil and gas, drilling company, Patterson-UTI Drilling company had engaged in patterns or practices of hostile work environment harassment, disparate treatment discrimination and retaliation against Hispanic, Latino, Black, American Indian, Asian, Pacific Islander and other minority workers at its facilities in Colorado and other states. These practices are against the democratic constitution's legislation. Yet cases of discrimination continue to prop up from time to time. But alright so these cases prove that racism against color and other ethnic discrimination exist in USA. But this fact cannot be denied that USA was formed by people who hailed from other countries where these and many more other types of discrimination were practiced. So those people brought these ideologies along with them to USA. Its true that while racism was practiced majorly by the earliest tyrant ones around the world and the earliest settlers in the land of the free the "WHITE people". But it was also practiced on a large scale by the Japanese against Chinese people and Korean people.

Romans owning their personal gladiators was a product of discrimination. What was SLAVERY? Slavery was the product of DISCRIMINATION. The rich oppressing the poor with their tyranny was a product of discrimination. Most popular religion CHRISTIANITY forcefully made others around the world to accept their faith by way of conversion, what was that? A product of discrimination. Today these ISLAMIC EXTREMIST JIHADIS massacring innocent people around the world is what? A product of discrimination. What evolves DISCRIMINATION is "HATE". The thirst to be considered SUPERIOR to others. While the fight for equality and the fight against racism is from almost the beginning of history, the fact is that for over 200 years Asian Americans have also been suffering the wrath of prejudice and racism in the western society. Even if they were not splashed as news highlights there are numerous cases when they were unreasonably imprisoned and denied justice. Indians, Chinese, Japanese and Koreans have all been fighting for equality for many years. Including in America, even though more focus prominence is given to African Americans, it's a fact that almost every ethnic group, every community and every race has at one point or another been targeted with attacks of racism. It's not that only communist countries censor and manipulate and designate the prominence and importance of news, shamefully even democratic countries do it.

The seeds of racism were sowed into the minds of white people even before they migrated into the AMERICAS from Europe. The idea of Africans as inferior, backwards and barbaric can be traced back to the times and era which justified slavery in the 18th century by tyrant and powerful ones.

Traveling back in time, we find many great people who have died doing all that they could to correct the wrong notions and understandings of the superiority and inferiority of humans. One of the greatest human being of all times, Mr. Abraham Lincoln, President of US during the American civil war. In the year 1863, it was he who declared *"that all persons held as slaves"* within the rebellious states *"are, and henceforward shall be free."* This declaration outlawed the practice and the belief of slavery. Then there is yet another remarkable personality, a former slave himself, Frederick Douglass(1818-1895), worked to end injustice of slavery and racism in America. He gave many stirring speeches criticizing injustice and raising the hope for a nation where all people were treated equally regardless of race, sex or religion.

The understanding about countries which were once upon a time proudly considered great because of their democratic policies and principles of respect for human rights and for respectfully practicing equality have tragically changed in the hearts and minds of people based upon the constant ongoing contradictory practices which has divided the people who were united by the sacrifices of some truly great human beings.

Mohandas K. Gandhi, a dark complexioned man born in India and educated in England, traveled to South Africa in early 1893 to practice law under a one-year contract as a young Indian lawyer. He was subjected to and refused to comply with racial segregation rules on a South African train and was forcibly ejected at Pietermaritzburg. This act of racism, was probably his moment of truth. The incident gave him that strength which made him begin a fight against injustice and defend his rights as a human being. His fight for equality as a human being and to co-exist without being subjected to prejudice. He was futurist in his thinking. He felt deep inside himself that this act of racism will not end at him. This act of tyranny and cruelty of injustice must be stopped before it engulfs the entire world's population which was different and not white. He was able to speak English and was well aware of the English culture and belief and had definitely seen others in similar situation in which he found himself. His courage needed an initiation to start a revolutionary movement and that incident which occurred with him gave him the courage and the power to stand against the mighty British. At that moment he lighted a candle of HOPE for the people of SOUTH AFRICA and showed them that these tyrants are not invincible and can be defeated. He gave them a realization that we are all children of and creation of the SAME GOD. Nobody is born superior to anybody. Nobody is born to serve anybody. But then he realized that these very tyrants were mistreating and unreasonably punishing and brutally massacring his own countrymen back in India. This is why after awakening the people of South Africa, he expanded his revolutionary movement against the British from SOUTH AFRICA to INDIA.

We cannot help but note the name of yet another great spirited man Mr. Nelson Mandela. He spent over twenty years in jail for his opposition to the racist apartheid system which excluded blacks from many areas of society in South Africa. It was not only non-whites who stood up against slavery and against racism. There have been great souls like William Wilberforce (1759 – 1833) – Campaigned against slavery, helping to outlaw slavery in Great Britain. The Slavery Abolition Act 1833, was passed three days after his death, and Mikhail Gorbachev who brought about the transition from Communism to democracy in the Soviet Union and Eastern

Europe. It was he who allowed Berlin wall to come down and introduced freedom of speech and promoted religious freedom.

It was not that there only MEN who were doing their part to change the world. There have been many women who have spent their entire life in trying to change the world. White women and black women have both contributed equally in the society when the world was struggling and trying to cope up with problems of racism and discriminations. But it is truly very unfortunate that the contributions of Black women to shaping and changing the world for the better are often minimized. A few names are Ella Baker, Josephine Baker, Daisy Bates, Sojourner Truth, Harriet Tubman, an escaped slave who dedicated her life to freeing other American slaves. She became the most famous of the "Conductors of the Underground Railroad." However the list of women who have contributed greatly in the fight and the movement against slavery and racism, does not end with just these great names. There are many more unsung heroes and great personalities who worked equally hard but they either sacrificed their lives or remain too involved in the physical contributions on the basic levels so they remained unaccounted in print.

Slavery has not spared any civilization in any part of the earth. The British invasion of India was a well-studied and very well-orchestrated and a systematic invasion. India, a densely populated place with long established civilizations, had a long history of contact with Europe. The main contact between Britain and India was in trade. This really began to develop during the 1600s, when the East India Company was created, a private company owned by wealthy and important figures in Britain. The Company had a monopoly of trade between Britain and Asia. The main goods traded were cotton, silk and tea. However, spices and gems were also important commodities. By the 1780s they had a lot of influence over all of the rulers of the southeast coast of India. They also ruled

Bengal. Bengal's large population and wealthy princes offered tremendous opportunities for the British East India Company and they built up their wealth and their military power there. British were known to be extremely planned slave drivers. They were so calculative and manipulative that they employed their troops and included the locals in them to ensure total control and dominancy over the people.

So racial profiling and abuse of humanity by some humans against other humans is nothing new. Many people around the world have suffered the brunt of this act of RACISM. How can one human in their sane mind consider another human's life to be of less value or of less importance based on how one looks or based on what's the skin color of a human? Today we can easily and comfortably ask such questions. But history is witness that such questions in the past have lead to mass massacre of large communities.

Dr. Martin Luther King's "Beyond Vietnam" address, given at New York City's Riverside Church on April 4, 1967, a year to the day before he was assassinated, echoes in the hearts and minds of people who respect his ideology even today. He made a difference because his ideology touched millions of hearts around USA and around the world. But ever wonder why did DR. MARTIN LUTHER KING say " I HAVE A DREAM?" What was that dream in reality? What did he actually mean? In today's times to survive and continue to evolve as a compatible and harmonious human society its imperative that we look back at history and learn from our erroneous understandings and misconceptions based on human prejudice and ego that in the past resulted in social unrest even in a country as great as USA with all the great unprejudiced principles of equality and respect for humanity. We are almost as divided from within today as we were in the 60s and the 70s. Only not officially and openly. Does color define beauty? Does physical appearance define cleanliness or uncleanliness in a person? Does color decide the inferiority or the superiority of a race? Why has color mattered so much in our human society? Let us explore the reasons and get to the core of this issue to understand what is it that does not let go away the COLOR ISSUE from the minds of humans around the world. Because the fight should be against inhumanity, against injustice, unfairness and for equality. Not for any particular race or group of people. Because if it is only for one ethnic race then it becomes a racist slur. Not only against injustice against the COLOR PEOPLE. If we choose to fight only for one group or one race then again we are being RACIST. YOU CANNOT HEAL ONE WOUND WITH ANOTHER WOUND.

Lets get science involved in this. Beginning with what's the composition of our skin, lets break up the contents of all skin types. We have learned these facts in schools and colleges etc that the darkest skin tones are found in tropical latitudes with open grassland, while areas further from the equator that are forested tend to favor lighter skin tones. Skin colors are a result of unique distribution of pigments throughout the body. Pigmentation is highly heritable, being regulated by genetic, environmental, and endocrine factors that modulate the amount, type, and distribution of melanins in the skin, hair, and eyes. Skin color also depends upon the size, number, shape, and distribution of melanosomes, as well as the chemical nature of their melanin content. The epidermis, the outermost layer of skin, provides a waterproof barrier and creates our skin tone. So we know that the skin's color is created by special cells called melanocytes, which produce the pigment melanin. Melanins compose a class of compounds that serve predominantly as a pigment. These pigments are derivatives of the amino acid tyrosine. So much for the skin types. About the hair structure, it is different in humans from different ethnicity, Hair structure is based upon the process of formation of the cells and genes in humans based on many environmental, climatic and other varied geographical aspects which when combined determine the type of skin and hair. Hair follicles are tiny pockets in our scalp out of which our hair grows. The thickness results from a combination of both the shape and size of the follicles, round, oval and flat and large and small. Large follicles produce thick hairs. Small follicles produce thin hairs. It is that simple. Follicles that are round in cross-section give rise to straight hair. Those out of which curly hair grows are oval. Very tightly coiled hair is due to the nearly flat, ribbon-like structure of the follicles. This hair texture is very common in people of African ancestry. The biological variations in humans do not determine the hierarchy of any one race. So this proves that skin colors or hair type in actuality have nothing to do with superiority or inferiority in social conditions. Its not that if you are light skinned you will be more successful or if you are dark skinned you are deemed to be a failure. The difference is in the psychological understanding of people about other people.

It is believed that if you belong to the same religion as another you are looked upon differently than those who do not belong to the common religion. Here color becomes completely irrelevant. Then again if two individuals work in the same place but there is no competition among them or if there is no disparity between them, color becomes irrelevant. If two people share the same ethnicity, culture, language but not religion then too color is not relevant. There could be other reasons for differences but not color for sure.

Can you imagine the world without the beautiful colors? How about the different seasons? Also what if there were no mountains, or waterfalls, different kinds of trees, plants and flowers? Why are there so many differences and variations in the climatic and environmental conditions in different parts of the world? Similarly there are so many biological, physical, and psychological differences in different species, which are all beautiful diversities created by the creator. But we can also look at these and every other diversity as discriminations. It's all about how you look at things.

Those people who considers themselves to be of superior race or more beautiful race and believe that other people whom they co sister to be inferior people should not even exist, need to understand the advantages and beauty from variations and diversities. Imagine if everyone in the world looked the same then what would be there to compare with? There would be nothing to appreciate or praise or choose or select or reject. Try painting your office walls and floor and ceiling all pure and plain WHITE. Now arrange the furniture also all WHITE and all identical. Now let there also be pure, bright, WHITE DAYLIGHT. Stay in that room for one hour. Note how you feel when you come out of that room and enter into a room that has multiple beautiful colors.

I wonder what gave this color discrimination such prominence that by the approach of the 21st century it spread around the world like wild fire and became so harmful and destructive in nature. The concept of "race" crystallized in late renaissance Europe at the dawn of the age of colonialism. Its purpose was to galvanize nation-states and to justify the abuses of colonialism. It was also a result of early psychological fear in humans against humans. Human beings have always been and still are inherently curious so their central concern specially in the past was whether the other human being is a friend or a foe. This can be best understood if we look at the history of native people who were less developed and less cultured, we are aware of how they were treated. Even though we were outsiders for them since they were the original settlers yet we treated them as outsiders. This was because of the fear in us for being considered and treated as outsiders. Racism is not an evolutionary trait. Racism is only a stimulant that boosts the ego of an individual or a community or a society to develop and grow and increase the size and strength of such people who believe in their right to practice these differences, which they use to control other human beings psychology and morale. Discrimination is also due to envious feelings from being jealous of other's prosperity and social and financial status.

Multiple small incidents in different pockets of cities and towns occur every now and then. Sometimes its the police, sometimes its some politician/senator and sometimes it is some business tycoon. Even after so many years of Dr King's departure if on one side there are people who remain ardent followers of his philosophy, principles and ideology, then on the other hand there are also people who remain unaffected and continue to practice racism.

Even though in many countries discrimination is orchestrated and purposely ignited and flared by political parties in a country by people with greed for political dominion and because of the greed to promote their political career. However all cases of discrimination are not for the same reason. Neither do they bear the same nature nor the same result. Some times discrimination is only out of fear and concern and is practiced as a PRECAUTION. Take for example the case of Europe. Recently Europe has displayed intolerance and discrimination towards Muslims based on the incidents from the deeds of Islamic extremists. "Muslim women are being denied jobs and girls prevented from attending regular classes just because they wear traditional forms of dress, such as the headscarf. Men can be dismissed for wearing beards associated with Islam." The entire European union comprising of Belgium, France, the Netherlands, Spain, and

Switzerland feels it is justified in adopt this new attitude towards Muslims. They find nothing wrong in taking precautions. What has been done by those who are discriminated to understand the reason of the discrimination? Whether something is wrong or it is right, there is always a REASON that would justify the acts of the doer to the doer. Many a times the discriminator alone is not completely to be blamed. But people find it easy to objectionably expose the impact of discrimination to gain sympathy or attention of the rest of the communities, just because they can and just because in general the world knows that it is wrong to discriminate. In case of Muslims, they have always expected and demanded the non-Muslims to understand Islam. What have they done to understand other faiths? Muslims complain about discrimination against them all over the world wherever they are. But how about the way they treat non-Muslims in their countries? Nobody has the right to question or challenge others if they are themselves practicing the same.

Many beliefs and practices may seem insignificant and nothing to be concerned about but in the practical world they are really discrimination. For example there are some religious society that are divisions of Christianity wherein they are actually told how to conduct your life and what to eat, what to wear etc. Women cannot wear make up or perfumes etc. They can neither enjoy parties or social events nor can they watch movie or even Television. All such cults separate those individuals from the rest of the world. Did God instruct those humans to live in this manner? These are mere interpretations or misinterpretations that have become a part of some religious beliefs and faiths. Such people avoid mingling with people outside their congregation. The result is that either they are discriminated against or they discriminate against others. They either consider themselves above others or think of others as of less significant. The seed of INEQUALITY doesn't always sprout from HATE. Some people become so involved and engrossed in following what they believe is from God that they cannot care to even realize that they are practicing inequality and discrimination. Only because they do whatever they do in the name of faith in God so to their understanding it is RIGHTEOUSNESS. They just don't have the care and understanding to realize that IGNORANCE IS NOT BLISS.

IGNORANCE is the key word in case of DISCRIMINATION. Ignorance of WHY ARE OTHER PEOPLE THE WAY THEY ARE. Which culture do they practice. People to whom anything about others is insignificant.

New Jersey in USA has a large population of Indians. In the Hindus people put a DOT on their forehead which has a very holistic meaning for them.

In 1987, there was this case of an Indian immigrant Mr Navroze Mody, who was a bank manager. He was unreasonably and brutally beaten to death by a gang which was chanting "Hindu, Hindu" with hatred filled in their hearts. This group called itself the "Dot Busters". It included teenagers too. The group had been targeting the hard-working community of

Indian immigrants with low-level harassment for months. The "dot" referred to the bindi which Hindu married women wear on their foreheads and also men who apply it on the forehead after prayers. Did they attack those people only because it was unclear as to why did those people wear the dots on their foreheads? No, of course not. It was because the group of people considered USA to be their country and therefore considered the more successful and prosperous Indian people to be outsiders and having come to USA they were snatching their share of the pie. The fact is that they are ignorant that here in USA everyone gets the opportunity to make their own pie and eat it too. Nobody is snatching anything from anybody. But its their understanding which develops due to their personal failure or due to the hatred in them for other people. There is no reasoning or justification for acts of hatred.

What about the incident when gunman stalked into a Sikh temple in Wisconsin, USA? They shot 6 people and wounded 3. The gunman's rampage ended when one of the police officers shot and killed him. Sikh community is from India and is a highly revered community in India. They were misunderstood to be Muslims even during the September 11 attacks had occurred. Its the ignorance of people who do not care to know about people from other communities from around the world, and based on their confused or wrong understanding of other people's culture, religion etc which makes them discriminate and look down upon others.

There is no one thing which triggers RACISM. There are numerous reasons why it exists even today. Like for example, a person may just not get a good vibe or one's own negative aura may repel against the other person's positive or negative aura. These are all natural phenomenon. Let's begin with FOOD which different societies eat. While today, almost everybody likes and enjoys the different varieties of food from different countries and cultures, there are many people who just eat what their taste glands are used and accustomed to. We have the right to like or dislike somethings. Specially FOOD. No one is wrong in having and expressing one's opinion.

British tyranny has barely spared any developing country or a country where they saw some potential for profit and growth. INDIA, SOUTH AFRICA, HONG KONG are just a few names. The scars from their tyranny are in many more parts of the world than just a few countries. Their influence and their impression made many others walk on the imprints of their footsteps. They are the original source of formation and creation of DISCRIMINATIONS. Today even though we presumably live in a humane, civilized and a democratic society, its only the face of the society that has changed. The HEARTS of some still continue to believe in tyranny being the right way. They do everything in their power to keep DIFFERENCES and DISCRIMINATIONS alive. Why do you think genuinely intelligent and well deserving geniuses and scholarly people are denied fairness? People of power give great speeches and talk about equality etc. But their actions don't always match their words. Why? But they find ways to justify everything that they do.

Until the source is revealed, all great work is enjoyed, appreciated and admired by everybody. However the moment the source is revealed, even today, the level of admiration and gratefulness comes down crashing. In the past, many great works of people not from the WHITE COMMUNITY, were either forcefully snatched from them or they did not get to see the light of the day. It was like only the White people had the authority over intelligence. But even so those who were destined to surpass all obstacles did move to the top. One such personality was this great African American artist MATT BAKER, from North Carolina, USA. He contributed a lot to the COMIC WORLD. The comics before him, did not have the same sensuous and romantic appeal which he introduced through his artworks. His contribution was unique for the world of Comic books.

Then of course how can we not remember MAYA ANGELOU, a legendary personality, again an African American woman. A woman of substance. She was a visionary writer who changed the image of the literary and the political world. She was one of key figures who started the CIVIL RIGHTS MOVEMENT. Then of course there was this great African American scientist, Percy Julian, whose contributions to the field of science through his research and development of synthetic compounds made him one of the most significant contributors to science and health care in the 20th century.

We will have to grow out of the recent rhetoric tensions and racial frustrations that the world is dealing with in current times. Instead of Protesting against racism we should be standing up against inequality. It's not only one community or society of people who are targeted. The attack is on humanity. The people who consider themselves of a SUPERIOR RACE are enemy of mankind and enemy of humanity. We have to unitedly fight against such atrocities which are products of egoistic and wrong beliefs and claims. Just like in the ancient past we humans have fought against all such forces which tried to destroy mankind and humanity. But humanity has always fought back and emerged victorious.

LIFE is life! People can be black, brown, yellow or white. It's the foremost responsibility of the parents to raise their children as HUMAN BEINGS who care for and respect HUMANITY. If we want to make this world a beautiful place where a mixed society with people from all walks of life and from country, ethnicity, social and religious background can breath the air with the same right, then we have to look at each other beyond our color, religion, language , culture, clothing etc. Parents and teachers can begin to sow the seeds of equality and better understanding in the tender minds of the next generation to change the future of mankind. How will our next generation look at and interact with each other in the future depends upon what we do today to make that change a reality. This is the only way to heal the wounds from inequality, racism, and every type of discrimination.

Science and religion can keep saying whatever they have to say. It is individuals who can and will have to work united to change hearts and minds. Recently there have been these slogans echoing in the atmosphere. Slogans like BLACK LIVES MATTER. While they are definitely cries with a request for love from the heart. What's concerning is why only BLACK LIVES? Why not LIFE IN GENERAL? Even though such slogans are drenched in tears based upon all the heartbreaking incidents that have occurred with people of color, the greatness of such slogans would have been a lot more if it included the tragic losses of life of others also. Because LIFE IS LIFE, we are all humans. Just because some people practice racism it doesn't mean others do the same. If by hurting back those who have hurt you your wounds would get healed then of course it could have been justified. But we are living in a civilized society not in the times when there were laws like AN EYE FOR

AN EYE, TEETH FOR TEETH or BLOOD FOR BLOOD etc.

Racial discrimination is definitely eye catching and alarming, but there are absolutely solid reasons for why they are housed by many hearts. There are differences even between people of one country, also based upon the hostility between their communities, or religions, etc in their country of birth which they are not able to let go of even after leaving their country. This is what gives birth to unhealthy competition and continues to maintain the hatred for one another. Now because of this if you stand out in a crowd, you will definitely draw attention and will naturally be subjected to the reaction and feelings of people who feel disgusted by your behavior and mannerisms.

Discrimination is practiced in workplaces even today. Many people can't help themselves from making it too obvious but when confronted or upon inquiring they out rightly deny and claim that their act was unintentional. Many others take undue advantage of their employee's need for their job and so the employer feels free to crack jokes with his/her racial slurs and comments.

Wherever there's a competition or a matter of choice for a higher level job or position and the candidates are both girls and boys, the priority and preference is given to a boy in most cases. The excuse or justification is "oh sooner or later the girl will have kids and her priorities will change!" Really? Won't the boy become a father too? Anyways this is not the end of discriminative acts. If a girl is not a white girl but an African American or an Asian or a Hispanic then the choice or competition just does not exist. Straight away a decision or a selection is made by the top authorities. If these women become pregnant they are in priority but very gradually and politely laid off. What can be said about male employees? In most cases, depending on the position, they are only entered in the competition to abide by the constitutional requirements. The result has already been decided.

Recently there was this case of a Muslim woman wearing a burka, who was thrown out of a big store in USA because of her appearance. She was covered from HEAD TO TOE only her eyes were visible. This flared up into a huge issue with objections from the Islamic community. But if we take a practical approach to this case and all other similar cases, we will find that somewhere the cause of the issue or the problem are the Islamic people. This may sound racist but not if you look at it in practical light. Because while it's a fact that reactions from fear n safety concerns are often unreasonable, it is also imperative to note and to understand that its also the responsibility of those people who are subjected to such reactions to avoid such incidents. With all due respects, pause for a moment and think, with all the ATROCITIES being committed by MUSLIM EXTREMISTS around the world by people who wear similar attire and practice the same faith and belief, how can you out-rightly point a finger on the acts from FEAR AND CONCERNS of those who do not know much about the cultures of other countries? Its obvious that the people who stand out will be looked upon with suspicion. It was the responsibility of the Muslim woman to be aware of the fact that she is not in her own society, where its a common and an everyday matter and a part of their life in their home country. WHY DO MUSLIM WOMEN WEAR HIJAB AND BURKA IN A FOREIGN LAND WHERE THERE ARE PEOPLE FROM MIXED MULTIPLE SOCIETIES AND CULTURES? Its easy to object and protest against voices that put forward their opinion, but the truth is that you are forcing to be DISCRIMINATED against.

EVERY ACTION IS A REACTION OF ANOTHER ACTION.
Until the time that terrorism exists and the you share the same exact customs and cultural practices SUCH INCIDENTS will continue. The BRUNT & the BURDEN of consequences that are a result of the acts of a community are often borne by those also who are innocent. You cannot be ignorant about the truth that

NOT EVERYBODY KNOWS ABOUT EVERY OTHER CULTURE. Their reaction IS PURELY based upon their ignorance but they alone cannot be blamed because you take others for granted expecting that they need to be aware of and respect your culture. IF YOU DON'T UNDERSTAND OTHERS HOW CAN YOU EXPECT OTHERS TO UNDERSTAND YOU? We live in a democratic society. The rights and responsibility is equally applicable for everybody.

Everybody talks about FREEDOM being very important and valuable etc but what exactly is freedom? Does freedom mean being able to ride a horse in the open field and shoot guns all around just because some folks love the firing sound? Or does freedom mean having people from around the world only to make a country look good from outside while inside every other person is chained and tied up with the chain of inequality and prejudice. Freedom also does not mean that one can do anything in the name of "rights". If you truly believe in freedom then inequality, disparity and racism would not exist in today's human society.

We need to find the sense of integrity in our lives and understand and respect the fact that others around us also have that and care for it. We all have to work towards self-restoration by realizing and practicing righteousness. Spend some time in nature, observe the nature and understand the magnificent technicality and the importance of everything in the nature for our existence. Release yourself from time constraints and immerse yourself in the wonders of being present and mindful of all that is happening within and around you. Care to realize that every one of us have a role to play and everyone of us make some contribution in the world in our own unique ways. Good or bad are consequences from unrealized and uncaring acts and are the results of frustration from rejection and failure, but even so everything and everyone exists for a purpose and acts in the way they do with a purpose. Without the existence of negativity we would not care to know and value righteousness and goodness. Not everybody is capable of realizing the consequences of one's doings but every can make an effort to implement habits that result in benefiting their mental, physical, and spiritual well-being. You don't have to denounce the world and become a yogi or a saint or a holy person, but you must certainly for a change at least once in your lifetime, try to practice for your own self love, attention, and care. If you cannot love yourself then the truth is that you can never love anybody and nobody will ever love you. You'll be surprised with the results from caring for your own body, mind, and soul. The changes will be so obvious and prominent in you that you will begin to notice the change in your own personality and this will give you feeling of immense joy.

The laws are necessary to maintain orderly society and therefore are to be understood as social rules and should not be looked upon as challenge to your rights just because they are enacted by authority. Every single and individual human being desires to have undisputed and unchallenged rights over joy, hope, gratitude, interest, serenity, pride, amusement, love. There's nothing wrong in practicing self compassion and self respect but humans are also a weak species and easily succumb to ego, false pride, anger and jealousy. Not everybody is powerful enough to gain control over these feelings/emotions.

Because they are caused in a natural and through a gradual process from family and internal or external stress, which are supported by feelings like regret, doubt and fear.

The entire world is aware that RACISM is a problem. But then why has it continued to exist in our society until this day? Just as you cannot heal a wound with another wound, similarly RETALIATION is never going to help resolve this problem. Those who strongly believe in racism feel a kind of contentment and satisfaction and even victorious in putting the other person down. They treat their success like an achievement when they feel they were able to put the other person in the place where they believe they rightfully deserve to be. Retaliation from agitation will lead to more agitation and attacks and result in bloodshed and social disorder and communal unrest. I cannot help but remember and mention a GREAT MAN'S QUOTE HERE:

"You must be the change you wish to see in the world.
The weak can never forgive. Forgiveness is the attribute of the strong.

Happiness is when what you think, what you say, and what you do are in harmony.
Live as if you were to die tomorrow; learn as if you were to live forever.
First they ignore you, then they laugh at you, then they fight you, then you win.
An eye for eye only ends up making the whole world blind.
Strength does not come from physical capacity. It comes from an indomitable will.
The best way to find yourself is to lose yourself in the service of others.
A man is but the product of his thoughts; what he thinks, he becomes.
You must not lose faith in humanity. Humanity is an ocean; if a few drops of the ocean are dirty, the ocean does not become dirty."

Racism is not the only form of discrimination which humans are subjected to and suffering from. Just like in the western world the people of dark skin and other non-white humans face the wrath of and are tortured with racial discrimination, in the most middle eastern countries, specially Saudi Arabia, Bahrain and Kuwait. The reason that many such news does not get out of these countries because of the manipulated and controlled media. Also these oil rich Islamic countries dominate and manipulate those countries that are dependent on their OIL and are forced to stay out and maintain silence to the atrocities and sufferings that the people living there are subjected to.

Discrimination against women is probably as old as the color discrimination if not older. It was only after 1919 that women got the right to vote in a country like USA which has always been looked upon by the rest of the world from the day it earned its independence. Prior to that the women were expected to stay at home and manage the kids and run the house. Education in the US favored males, but by 1870 grade school was free in the US. Women had very little rights, few property rights, rights to divorces and often got the short end of the stick. African-American women on the other hand where treated on average worse than other races of women or white women. People of color were always considered lowest in western world on a social scale.

Another very prominent discrimination is religious. This is a very common fact that today every single religion is doing everything in its power to increase and have as many more number of believers and followers on their side. No matter in which part of the world, if there's an area which is dominated by people of a particular religion, if the people from other religions become a part of the minority community, they are forced to either accept their religion or leave that area or die. This is not just in countries like BANGLADESH, PAKISTAN, INDIA or CHINA, but also in the middle eastern countries. For instance, even though Bahrain is majorly a SHIA STATE, the Muslims in Bahrain are practically ruled by the SAUDI SUNNIS. The SHIA and SUNNI issue is a huge discriminatory issue in the Islamic society. Just like the Roman Catholic church and the Protestant CHURCH ISSUES. Even though the issue between Roman Catholics and Protestant Christians is not as huge as SHIA-SUNNI issue, it is a very concerning issue which can escalate into a bigger issue someday. What about the religious suppression by China on the Christians and other religious communities in China? Chinese government believes the church members to be of dangerous cult. They were charged with using cult to challenger the government's laws.

The truth is that EVERY DISCRIMINATION cannot be fought against or erased from our society ever. It may begin from misunderstandings that attack people's ego, but once egos are hurt the problem becomes permanent and an inseparable part of the human society. Another example to prove this is the caste system in India. In the days of the kings the utterly poor and socially weak chose to do the leftover kind of jobs that nobody else was willing to take up. Like the job of transporting the human wastes and keeping the sewage clean. Cleaning the animal skin after the kings killed the animals in sport. People who did any work involved in or related with touching or preparing leather from animal skins. So the people who did take up those types of jobs were called UNTOUCHABLES or people of low caste. Even after so many centuries and millenniums, even though they newer generations of those people are no longer involved in doing such jobs, they are still considered of LOW CASTE. The government of India has tried and did a lot to uplift such socially rejected and looked down upon people, but even the most educated people in India continue to practice their ancestral beliefs and practices. Regardless of in which country in which form discrimination is practiced, the point is that not every discrimination is due to hurting of egos. Much of the discrimination is practiced intentionally and out of choice, being completely aware of how much it hurts a person deep within and how it effects and impacts the psychology of others.

We are all humans and even though our soul is a fragment of a fraction of the GOD energy but we have a similar nature. It is not only humans who discriminate. What about the fact about some humans being born blind, mute, and disabled? Yes to some extent, in some cases it may be due to malnutrition or environmental conditions or life conditions of those humans. But what about the other cases which are naturally existing from birth? Then those other facts of some people becoming extremely wealthy due to luck factor without having to do much. While some people continue to struggle all their life just to survive and some people die from hunger and poverty or because they are unable to afford medical facility. The people living in a better conditioned society cry about being discriminated because they find other people posing difficulties and creating obstacles in way of their advancements in life. But even they discriminate against the people who are less fortunate in life than them. So how can we blame anybody at all? Who should we blame? Why do we expect that a miracle will happen and suddenly everything will get fixed by itself some how some day? God is in us and we have the power to change ourselves and our life conditions. We have the power to change our nature of thoughts, actions and deeds. Just as Mahatma Gandhi had said IF WE WANT TO SEE THE WORLD AROUND US CHANGE, THEN WE HAVE TO BE THE CHANGE.

Those who are ardent believers of racism are not more than those who are victimized. Changes don't occur overnight. If you really intend to erase the problem and if you want to see the world change then it has to begin from you. Waiting for others to take the first step is a completely wrong decision. Dreaming for a change alone is not enough. Nothing happens by itself. To change the world you have to change yourself first. Every major social change demands great sacrifices. How much can anybody put you down? For how long can they go on if you don't retaliate? By retaliating you are encouraging them to continue to do it. Because their intention in doing the acts and in speaking the words is to hurt your psychology and morale and retaliation is the reaction that they want from you. Before this problem is erased from our society, there will be many who will have lost their lives. But these sacrifices will not go down the drain. The world that you will be giving to your children and to the children of your children will be a much safer, caring, understanding, loving, and humanely a better world. We could not have seen this day in USA had it not been for that ONE MAN'S DREAM – Dr Martin Luther King.

When the election times arrive people show enthusiasm and go to vote. They vote for someone based on some qualities in that person that appeals to the people. But after being elected when their expectations are failed and they are betrayed what do people do? They turn around and ask WHAT CAN WE DO? Well the person you voted for and empowered to govern your country and you has everything that was given to him/her by you. What do you do when you give a toy to your child and he/she hurts himself/herself or someone else with it? You immediately take it away from the child. You create a monster and then complain about the damages he/she does?

The problems in our society are self inflicted. The beauty of diversity created by God to make the world a beautiful place for living beings, was converted by mankind into a tool against mankind to hurt others and to divide mankind. God created only one beautiful RACE of human beings with beautiful diversities of colors, features, shapes and sizes. When you are a little child what is your nature, or culture, or community, or a society or a religion? Whether in humans, or in animals or in birds, observe little babies and note the changes that they go through as they grow up. Why are they not able to differentiate between color or language or caste or community or anything? It is the grown ups who directly or indirectly feed every difference in them over the period. somethings sometimes intentionally and many a times many things are fed into them unintentionally.

The blame is solely on the way that one practices one's culture and how does one carry oneself around in the society. There was a time when people found the style, mannerisms and behavior of African-American people not befitting in the white people's society. If you observe today, you can see everywhere, people from every ethnicity and country following the style and mannerisms of the African-American people. Its not that previously the white society did not consider them civilized or cultured and now they do. No. There are many people who still continue to look upon them as if they are some primitive people. They conveniently ignore the great African-American people who established themselves as highly regarded and respected personalities in almost every field. But even so that image about them continues to follow them. This is because the African countries from where their ancestors hailed are not as developed as many other countries even to this date. But is it fair to continue to put even the modern day African-American people in the same category as their ancestors? Of course not. This notion and misconception needs to be changed. Because even though the African countries may not be rich and wealthy and technologically advanced like many other countries, they are earthy people. Them being untamed or uncivilized and uncultured is how all humans were billions of years ago. They keep us connected to and remind us of our origin, from where we all started our journey of humanity.

Somehow or the other people find a way to hold something against others around them. Today people from every country have something or the other against people from other countries. If it's not the success and social advancement then it's either skin color or religion or language, customs or against just their general behavior.

The pain from the wounds of racism and other discrimination makes the person so nervous that he/she looses confidence and remains defensively extra careful and alert always. They are forced to think that they are not the personality which they believed they were. There's no realization of the need to reconcile and erase the differences among people of today.

Humans have the time and the patience to tolerate and bear with their animal friends like cats, dogs and even with wild creatures like SNAKES, LIONS, TIGERS, CROCKEDILE and even with many insects. Because they do not argue, or go against your will, or show you attitude, or do not pose any threat of competition. You have some how accepted that you are superior than them and that they are in no way ever going to endanger your existence ever.

There are many simple and ordinary looking ways that forcefully establish a WRONG as RIGHT. For example look at the case of Marathon race. In a marathon race, there are hundreds of people from almost all over the world and from almost every country who participate. But eventually there can be only one winner. The pace of life for everyone has increased so much that in today's times every individual is running. Nobody wants to loose, everybody wants to be a winner. In a race there is no compromise. Everybody gives their utmost best. But then when somebody is favored over others by the judge's personal choice and preference who either disqualify a true and a sincere athlete for favoring another person with unjustifiable and unreasonable margins, it hurts and breaks even the best athlete. But then after a few fusses and hues and cry everything goes back to normal and the same incident continues to be repeated over and over again until the general public begins to believe in the wrong way to be the right one. Nobody ever wants to admit committing a wrong when the wrong is executed with the intention of establishing the supremacy of people from one type of society, community, ethnicity, group or religion. Marathon is only an example, but this applies to every field in the world, wherever there is a possibility of competition between people from different societies, communities, ethnicity and religions etc.

Everything has a beginning. Many a times simple factors create much bigger issues. Things usually begin from a MATTER OF CHOICE. That matter of choice could be the first sparks of that fire which could soon consume an entire society. Somewhere back in time, discrimination may have been a matter of choice for somebody or for a small group of individuals. As the concept of A MATTER OF CHOICE spreads and begins to have an impact and influence over other people around you and other regions around the world, it develops into a global issue. When people try to illegibly establish by any possible means, their matter of choice as a commonly accepted phenomenon, even when their choice is not synchronized with other people's choice or acceptance, it invokes protests, communal unrest and social disorder, inflicting problems upon innocent lives who have never had experience of any such issues. Observe a WILD animal that is cornered by hunters or scavengers and when there's no escape it retaliates and fights back. This is what those humans did who were discriminated against and suppressed, dominated and enslaved by tyrant, unfair, unjust people from powerful societies for centuries. There comes a time in every person's life when bearing with unfairness, injustice, unacceptable and unreasonable and unnecessary tyranny becomes impossible. This is when the oppressed stands his/her ground and says ENOUGH IS ENOUGH. This is how revolutions begin. This is how changes begin to appear in the society. This is how the society of people who've always considered themselves superior to others have forced the discriminated, the suppressed and the oppressed people to stand up to demand for their rights. Why should we continue to suffer prejudice, discrimination, or antagonism only because some humans want to continue to believe that their own race is superior to all others? Each race possesses characteristics or abilities specific to that race which makes them unique in their own rights. Their qualities distinguish them to be recognized as yet another race or races. But the qualities of characteristics and or abilities don't determine whether one race is superior to another or inferior to another. Why is this simple phenomenon continued to be challenged even today? Complex interactions between societies and communities have existed from the time that time count itself began. History is witness, we have read about and studied about the violent treatment that different races have suffered time and again in different forms. The modern society of today has emerged by defeating the religious tyranny, racial, gender, class discriminations. But it appears like the cleanup of such understandings and beliefs did not vanish completely. It is the residue which is suffocating us and with which we have to fight today. We have no option but to defeat them and emerge victorious. Only then we will be able to provide to our future generations a better world to breath in.

Enough has been written about and said about the need and essence to care for and to accept the need for understanding the right of equality in every individual's life. In our beautiful world. It hurts to see that the newer generation is also getting caught up in the ongoing problems of inequality and racism. Looking at the way the world is today, the way people are treating people, taking pleasure in putting the other one down, laughing at other's pain and leaving the wounded to suffer the agony and the misery of prejudice, I remember Louis Armstrong sing with a smile on his lips and with pain in his heart which he couldn't help escape through his voice and touch every soul, every time it plays. It was a reminder, then and it remains a reminder even today for every heart to realize "WHAT A WONDERFUL WORLD" we live in. But just like he says I too see friends shaking hands, but I know all they are saying is I am better than you. With humans continuing to suffer so much pain for so many hundreds of years now, I wish that the wounds get healed. I wish that we can look into each other's eyes and really say that yes, it is a wonderful world. Just like a building maybe beautiful with the most modern amenities and facilities but it only becomes a beautiful home when people begin to dwell in it, similarly the world has everything in it to make it a beautiful place. Only we the people need to stop considering other people as inferior and enemies or of less significance. These beliefs and understandings can never let the world ever be a wonderful place. The colors today are only pretty in the rainbow in the sky. The same colors when seen on earth in people's lives are wounded and tainted and are no longer considered beautiful and worthy of appreciation. I truly wonder and am patiently waiting for the day when for the sake of those few souls who are trying their best in their own special ways to revive humanity, and for the sake of the future generations, I'd be able to say "yes, Respected Louis Armstrong, yesterday you thought, and today I think, it is after all A WONDERFUL WORLD!

  Hatred among mankind is increasing and spreading. Religion and racism and on the fore front but they lead to many other different kinds of prejudice. We are witnessing mass murder of humans in the name of religion by the Islamic extremists but that's because the nature of their operation is too violent and the incidents occur too often and are publicly known. But there are other discriminations and issues that are practiced in disguise, covered and with pretentions so the effects are not clearly noticed and understood. Racism in American is huge problem today. It may not sound right when the whole community or a race is tainted and labeled as some stereotyped people, but its not completely baseless when it is done. Because based on behavioral and social statistical study and criminal records it has been found that black men and Mexicans do commit more crimes than white men and Asians. However even so it does not get justified that the entire race of African-Americans and Mexicans be put into the same slot. It is however also the responsibility of the rest of the people of a society and or community to make sure that they do understand rationally the reason of why their people are targeted. This applies to people of different race and of different faith also. Because Religion is the oldest routine that harms both, the religious community and the faithful when you deny people the rights to practice their faith. It is also true that the faithful need to respect considerately and care to remain aware of the existence of others who do not practice or know about other or all religions. Also expecting others to understand one's faith, mannerisms, religion or religious deity has been a great cause for feuds and violence.

Recent brutality cases by police on black people has raised many eyebrows and opened many mouths loud in shock. But Just like not all black men are criminals so also it is true that not all cops are racists. Yes we live in a democratic society so we all have the rights to have our opinion about the world around us. But that does not mean we become judgmental about others

based on a few or a lot of incidents labeled on their people. There are good and bad people in every race, community, society, religion and country. Some may have less of problematic people some may have a lot of them. News about other races flashes immediately in the controlled media of today. What about the recent cases where innocent black men were shot dead with no remorse or regret by white police? The white conservatives are fully supportive of what the cops did in New York, Missouri, Illinois, California, Arizona and other states where white officers/deputies shot and killed an unarmed black person. Conservatives maintain a double standard about use of police force on Blacks.

The impact on the psychology and the morale of the victims of racism and other forms of discrimination is a wound which their entire personality. It damages their confidence in themselves and their faith in God. In many cases based on their individual experience and the magnitude of the impact it starts a chain of reactions and acts against others around them engulfing and targeting only the innocent people just like they were when they were targeted at first.

Today even though people have become more aware of the fact that racism in general is illegal, and punishable by law, even then many people, including many of the law enforcement officers practice discriminations like racism like a cult.

They justify to themselves their own acts as a way to punish the trespassers and infringers and intruders. The land of the FREE SPIRITED HUMANS is being claimed by some people as their ancestral property when it clearly is not. They forget that just like every single other immigrant, their ancestors also came to this LAND OF THE FREE SPIRITED from somewhere with dreams and ambitions in their hearts to make this land as their home country.

   Just like if you boarded a public bus or a train a few stations before others doesn't make the bus or the train your personal property so also just because your ancestors made this LAND OF THE FREE SPIRITED their home before other people made it their homes, the land of the free does not become the belonging of anybody. So why should there be a need to repeat the words of the founding fathers to fight against and to stop racism?

   Criminals and offenders find their ways to exist in every society. But based on their nature of actions and treatment of the society we cannot and should not create a general consensus about every member of a society to be criminals and offenders. It cannot be justified ever and cannot be accepted as fair or just. But this has become the trend in recent times by those who ardently believe that they are a higher race or the better or the more beautiful race among humans. Today even the

higher authorities are involved in abusing the law and in challenging the constitutional principles of our country - The Land of the free. These people are those who bear responsible position in the society to protect the rights and respect and the honor of the day to day civilians. They are the ones who are approached by the regular civilians in troubled situations to seek protection and justice. In many cases sufferings from prejudice proves worst than physical injuries.

It is definitely hurtful that some people can bring themselves to think of and make somebody forcefully to believe that they are of less importance and that they are a less significant race? But what's even more hurtful is that they feel no guilt or remorse and regret from their thoughts and actions. We have all suffered hurt from some injury at some point in time and so we know what is PAIN. Just imagine yourself to be in love with somebody and he/she rejects you for what you are because of what you are. Later on in life even if you do find love that hurt and pain from rejection does not get erased from your mind. They will always remain conscious and will always be defensive about who or what they are. They'll never be able to give their best to anything, they'll never be able to feel good about themselves.

So is there anything like a superior race? There are many reasons why the complexity of superiority and inferiority of human race exists in our society.

Chronicle study about ancient humans, tells us that the biological variations in our human genes is from the ancient relationships that existed among different kinds of human like species and humans.

  Research study has determined that DNA, or deoxyribonucleic acid, is the molecule that makes up an organism's genome in the nucleus of every cell which consist of molecular codes that regulate the output of genes. To a great degree the different impressions about how similar chimpanzees and humans are is also a cause of one human's treatment of another human based on their appearance or behavioral patterns or the nature of instincts. Scientists could spend their entire lifetime in researching and studying to find and prove to the world that we have evolved from APES or CHIMPANZEES etc, and I tell you they'll never reach a conclusion. Because we have not. Such assumed studies and speculated presentations and then pin pointing the place from where all mankind originated and then spread across the globe is giving false notions and understanding and could lead some people to believe as their race to have completed the process of evolution and become completely humans while others are still in the process of evolution.

We have accepted to become dependent upon scientific presentations and acclamation of all kinds because 60% of the times their material studies and findings and presentations have proved to be accurate. This is why we accept even their speculated and presumptuous presentations as accurate and apply it in our life basing our judgements on our understanding of those presentations. Dependency in any form is wrong. Speculation of any kind is wrong. Understandings can be forced in to people. Not everybody is a scientist. Not everybody can understand scientific research works to be able to question or to challenge the works and presentations of the scientists. The dominating authorities in countries remained concerned about success in governing and finding solutions to prevailing problems and issues. So the scientists are on their own with nobody to question or to challenge their claims. But who bears the brunt and suffers the wounds from their speculations and claims? The day to day human being. Who gets blamed for carrying the torch of racism?

It is the day to day human beings of course.

However anybody may try to provide as many facts as possible in as best way as possible, or as clearly understandable as possible, changes will only come by acceptance of our own wrong practices, habits, mannerisms, language, clothing, way of reacting to whatever we say or hear or do. Its our responsibility to notice in ourselves what others notice in us. Its for us to see what do others object in us. Its up to us to understand why do others object to our ways at all. Its us who need to realize and understand that today everywhere we may go, the world is a mixed up society. There are people from other cultures, who speak other languages, who wear other type of clothes. They sing differently, they dance differently. The old saying and proverbs in their culture are different than yours. They may be applying and following different philosophy in life. Yes they are as human and as humane as you are but you all are STRANGERS to one another. If we want the world to be a better place. Then we have to understand that NOBODY OWNS THE WORLD. GOD IS THE SOLE

PROPRIETOR OF THE UNIVERSE.
Today we are here tomorrow someone else will be here. All existence is perishable and temporary and has an expiry date. But there's no expiry date for GOD. It is with this understanding that we should to be willing to establish acquaintance with each other on the basis of respect, care, consideration, compassion, kindness, regardless of where you have come from. What matters is WHERE YOU ARE GOING TO SPEND THE REST OF YOUR LIFE. What matters is that the society which you are also a part of are there not because you have chosen them to be but because you have chosen to become a part of an already existing society. At the same time you have to know that everybody in this society is here because they have chosen to make themselves a part of this society. Nobody is SUPERIOR, nobody is SENIOR, nobody is special, and nobody is INFERIOR.

We are ONE SPECIES, ONE RACE, THE RACE OF HUMAN BEINGS. We are all created by the same CREATOR with all our variations, diversities, and qualities. We are all UNIQUE in our own ways. Whether we realize or not, we all have a purpose for which we are existing. The hurts from our pursuits, from our words, the slurs, acts of discrimination, and the deeds of racism give to humanity, wounds beyond repair. Our variations, our qualities, our diversities are the HUMAN RAINBOW with beautiful colors. Do not hurt or harm, do not inflict pain. Let us all do just our part in helping heal the WOUNDS OF COLOR.

AYE JAHAAN KYA TERI NAZAR KA MUSTAHIQ HUN MAIN
USI IK RAB NE BANAYA MUJHAY BHI TERI TARAH
DHADKANAY DIL KI PADHATI HAIN DUWA SHAAM-O-SUBAH
KYA HUWA GAR MERI ZUBAAN NAHI HAI TERI TARAH

MAINAY DEKHA HAI AASHIYAANO KO JALTAY HUWAY
KHUDAA KE NAAM PE WEHSHAT KO ZULM KARTAY HUWAY
POOCHHA MANDIR AUR MASJID SAY MAAJRAA KYA HAI
SABHI KEHTAY HAIN ROOHDAAR HAIN SUB TERI TARAH

PIGHALTAY MOAM JAISAY BHOOK SE NANGAY BACHCHAY
AANKHON MAIN SOOKHAY AANSOO LIYE BEBUS MAAYAIN
KYN TOD BAITHEE HAIN UMMEED SE SAARAY RISHTHAY
KABHI INKAY BHI DIL MAIN IK KHUDAA THHA TERI TARAH

JISNAY MAKHLOOQ BANAYI WOH ISHQA WAALA KHUDAA
KHOON KE PYAASAY IS WEHSHY KHUDAA KA KOYI NAHI
MAGHFIRAT KAISAY HOGI AISAY GUNEHGAARON KI
OONCHHAY DARBAAR MAIN YEH NA HONGAY TERI TARAH

www.ingramcontent.com/pod-product-compliance
Lightning Source LLC
Chambersburg PA
CBHW070200290526
45789CB00002B/851